D0353825

POCKET PAL
MULTIPLE INTELLIGENCES

MIKE FLEETHAM

Illustrations by Mike Phillips

B L O O M S B U R Y
LONDON · NEW DELHI · NEW YORK · SYDNEY

Bloomsbury Education

An imprint of Bloomsbury Publishing Plc

50 Bedford Square	1385 Broadway
London	New York
WC1B 3DP	NY 10018
UK	USA

www.bloomsbury.com

Bloomsbury is a registered trademark of Bloomsbury Publishing Plc

First published 2007 by Continuum International Publishing Group

This edition published 2014 by Bloomsbury Education

Text © Mike Fleetham, 2007
Illustrations © Mike Phillips, 2014

British Library Cataloguing-in-Publication Data
A catalogue record for this book is available from the British Library.

ISBN: PB: 978-1-4729-0963-3
ePub: 978-1-4729-0965-7
ePDF: 978-1-4729-0964-0

Library of Congress Cataloging-in-Publication Data
A catalog record for this book is available from the Library of Congress.

1 3 5 7 9 10 8 6 4 2

Typeset by Newgen Knowledge Works (P) Ltd., Chennai, India
Printed and bound in Great Britain by Ashford Colour Press Ltd

This book is produced using paper that is made from wood
grown in managed, sustainable forests. It is natural, renewable
and recyclable. The logging and manufacturing processes conform
to the environmental regulations of the country of origin.

To view more of our titles please visit www.bloomsbury.com

Since the first edition of this book in 2007, a lot has happened: global recession, flood, war, famine and continued threats to the world's security and health. Now more than ever we need creative thinking and innovative solutions. Multiple Intelligences is a framework for this; for thinking differently, for learning in new ways. But most of all it's a way to leave no stone unturned in the quest that all educators follow: the search for that one thing that each child does best.

Everybody is intelligent. Everybody is valuable. Everybody succeeds.

CONTENTS

7

MI in your organisation

8

Find out more

INTRODUCTION

Is this book for you?

Yes, if you are someone who:

- Wants to make their teaching outstanding.
- Wants to get better at helping others to learn, grow and achieve.
- Believes in the potential of each human being to succeed.
- Is short of time but is keen to learn.
- Wants to understand and use the concept of multiple intelligences.

What the book offers

Simple, practical and quick ways to:

- Liven up any curriculum.
- Understand, talk about and use multiple intelligences.
- Find out how your learners are clever and how to value them.
- Give your teaching space a dynamic makeover.
- Enrich your planning, teaching and assessment.
- Improve your thinking, problem solving and creativity.
- Bring new ideas into your organisation.

How to read the book

You know your own reading style, but here are some suggestions:

- It's a short book; you could probably read the whole thing in an hour.
- Pick a chapter from the contents page that interests you.
- Just look at the diagrams and illustrations.
- Read the bulleted or numbered lists.
- Discuss the book with a colleague or friend.
- Go straight to the practical suggestions.
- Highlight ideas that catch your imagination.
- Highlight ideas that you question or want to know more about.
- Get the big picture from the map on the following page.

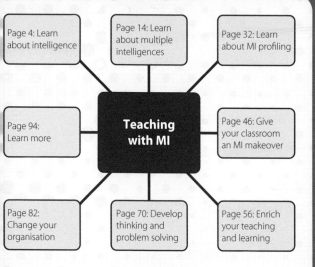

What is MI?

Multiple intelligences (MI) is a powerful and empowering tool for teaching and learning.

It describes, values and uses people's unique strengths, thereby helping people to work and learn more effectively. It is a spiral (rather than a straight line or a closed circle) along which you can move at your own pace, and where each stage of learning grows from the one before and leads into the next.

Once you understand the theory of MI, you'll discover many straightforward and practical ways to use it, and find many ways to express what you already know:

Everyone is good at something.

General intelligence – g

g (similar to IQ) is the overall mental ability that you use to get a score on a WAIS III assessment (Wechsler Adult Intelligence Scale, version 3). The assessment consists of 13 separate tests covering four broad areas of:

Verbal comprehension

for example, knowing what certain words mean.

Perceptual organisation

for example, completing a sequence of shapes.

Working memory

for example, remembering a sequence of numbers.

Processing speed

for example, working out the meanings of symbols under a time limit.

The results of the assessment suggest:

- Scoring well in one of the 13 tests is a pretty good indication that you'll do well in the others.
- The better your scores the more intelligent you are.
- High intelligence is reserved for those people who happen to perform well in the four areas tested.
- High intelligence is denied to those people who happen to excel in other ways.

For more, visit www.intelligencetest.com.

The concept of multiple intelligences (MI) is a highly effective way to think about 'being clever', but it's not the only way. This chapter discusses three other ideas about intelligence and the results of taking on each one.

...IN ACTION

Try these three problems similar to those used in measuring **g.**

Verbal comprehension

Which two words are closest in meaning?
> *shrewd, devious, clever, average, educated, attentive*

Perceptual organisation

Which shape is different from the others?

Working memory

One sequence at a time, say these number sequences out loud, close the book, then repeat them backwards.

4 – 7
1 – 5 – 3
2 – 8 – 5 – 3
3 – 9 – 5 – 4 – 1
8 – 5 – 7 – 3 – 4 – 3

Of course, with questions like these, it can be quite annoying not to be given the answers …!

Carol Dweck's Self-theory

Carol Dweck, Professor of Psychology at Stanford University, has discovered a fascinating and immensely important fact:

Learners' beliefs about their own intelligence can help determine their levels of success.

Incrementalists believe that intelligence can be learned – people can become cleverer. They believe that their efforts will make a difference, that problems can be overcome, and that learning, however difficult, will pay off.

Entitists believe that intelligence is fixed – whatever happens, they'll never be cleverer. They believe they can do little to improve their lot. Problems and difficulties are confirmation of their biological limitations.

If you adopt this self-theory, then:

- People tend towards being either entitist or incrementalist.
- Within this range, those around you will have different beliefs about their intelligence and abilities to learn.
- What you say to your learners and how you say it will reinforce their self-belief.

For more, see *Mindset: How You Can Fulfill Your Potential* (Robinson, 2012).

> **TIP:**
> Incrementalist or entitist? Self-belief appears to be fixed at the age of three, and is mainly down to parental expectations.

...IN ACTION

Listen to your learners and colleagues over a set period of time. Be alert for key phrases that might indicate self-belief.

Tick the boxes if you hear these or similar examples. **Note:** *Do* think carefully about what you hear – these examples are not in context.

Incrementalist

☐ How are we going to solve this?
☐ I'm learning to …
☐ What choices do we have?
☐ How can we work with what we've got?
☐ I expect …
☐ I hope that …
☐ We can …
☐ Let's have a go
☐ *Carpe diem*
☐ I'm clever

Entitist

☐ I can't …
☐ We'll never get to the end of this
☐ It's one initiative after another
☐ They're always telling us what to do
☐ It won't work
☐ *C'est la vie*
☐ There's no point
☐ You'll never manage it
☐ We have no choice

Remember not to judge people for their self-belief. This exercise is designed to hone your skills of recognising how people see themselves. Incrementalist is no better or worse that entitist and the same person may switch between the two in different circumstances.

David Perkins' Intelligence theory

David Perkins, professor of education at Harvard University, believes that:

Intelligence can be taught and learned.

He identifies three different kinds of intelligence:

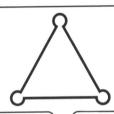

Neural intelligence:
the brain's raw processing power

Experiential intelligence:
knowledge acquired by doing

Reflective intelligence:
learning new ways to solve problems and self-monitoring these strategies

Perkins' ideas suggest that:

- Everyone can become more intelligent.
- You can teach intelligence to your learners – by providing experiences and problems to solve.
- High intelligence is available to more people than with **g** (experiential intelligence).

For more, see *Outsmarting IQ: The Emerging Science of Learnable Intelligence* by David Perkins (The Free Press).

TIP:
David Perkins says: "We can become more intelligent through study and practise, through access to appropriate tools and through learning to make effective use of those tools."

...IN ACTION

Write down answers to these three questions:

Name one thing that you can do really really well (in any aspect of your life – work, learning, family, social, relaxation).

How did you learn to do this thing?

How do you know that you can do it really really well?

The chances are that your responses to these questions prove (under David Perkins' theory) that you have become more intelligent at some point in your life.

Howard Gardner and MI

Howard Gardner's theory of multiple intelligences encompasses, integrates and enhances the three theories we've just looked at.

Through his work with brain-damaged patients in the early 1980s, Gardner discovered an interesting phenomenon:

When specific brain areas are damaged, specific sets of skills and talents disappear, while others remain intact.

This led Gardner to develop the notion that in each human brain, there are several different kinds of mind.

In the theory, each 'mind' has a distinct intelligence which drives a particular set of human abilities.

To begin with, Gardner came up with seven intelligences:

Logical/mathematical

Verbal/linguistic

Interpersonal

Intrapersonal

Visual/spatial

Bodily/kinesthetic

Musical/rhythmic

In the mid-1990s, Gardner added an eighth:

Naturalist

And over recent years he has considered one more:

Existential

But he hasn't discovered enough evidence for it, so the current official count is eight and a half intelligences.

For more, see Howard Gardner's book *Intelligence Reframed: Multiple Intelligences for the 21st Century* (Basic Books).

...IN ACTION

Link these activities to the pictures representing the intelligences. (Some may link to more than one picture; some may link to none.)

Linguistic

Existential

Logical

Visual

Naturalist

Bodily

Intrapersonal

Interpersonal

Musical

Singing
Composing
Listening
Talking
Writing
Debating
Wondering
Classifying
Balancing
Coordinating body
Collaborating
Thinking
Controlling body
Empathising
Being self-motivated
Reasoning

11

MI in summary

There are eight and a half equally valuable ways to be clever. Between them they cover the full range of human potential, skill and talent.

Each intelligence has had to pass eight rigorous tests to earn the right to be part of MI theory and practice. A candidate intelligence must:

1. Have a core set of skills and talents.
2. Lead to specific careers.
3. Have grown as humankind has evolved.
4. Be testable by psychologists.
5. Have psychometric tests* for it.
6. Have a symbol system.
7. Appear as a special need or gift in certain people.
8. Link to specific brain areas.

The eight full intelligences meet these criteria, but existential does not yet. Neither do spirituality, morality, humour … windsurfing or shopping!

If you think of intelligence in terms of Gardner's theory:

- Everyone is intelligent in their own unique way.
- There are at least eight ways to be clever.
- Intelligences are used in combination.
- Everyone has all intelligences but to different levels.
- Everyone can improve any intelligence within certain limits.

MI doesn't contradict **g**, IQ or other views of intelligence, but over the last 20 years or so it has stirred up the debate about what is meant by being clever. Many people are uncomfortable with such a broad definition – usually folks with very high **g**! Many others warmly embrace MI's potential to help people value themselves for who they are and what they can become.

It's your choice – what is intelligence to you and your learners?

***

* A psychometric test is a structured way to measure mental ability and/or personality.

...IN ACTION

Discover the wide range of beliefs about intelligence and open up a discussion with your learners. Ask them these questions:

Are you …?

1. Not very clever at all
2. Fairly clever
3. Clever
4. Very clever
5. Extremely clever

Who is the cleverest person you know?

[ ]

What makes him or her so clever?

[ ]

A year from today, will you be cleverer than you are now?

1. No way.
2. Maybe.
3. Yes.

If someone is clever, they can (tick the four most important things):

☐ Write neatly
☐ Do maths
☐ Help other people
☐ Remember things
☐ Work quickly
☐ Solve problems
☐ Do puzzles
☐ Finish first
☐ Talk clearly
☐ Play an instrument
☐ Paint and draw
☐ Play a sport
☐ Write poems
☐ Make and keep friends

IDEA...

Visual/spatial intelligence

Nickname: **Picture Smart**

Area of the brain: **Visual cortex, right hippocampus and parietal cortex**

Your potential to think in images and to understand how objects fit and move together in the real world.

> An artist is a dreamer consenting to dream of the actual world.
>
> *George Santayana*

Typical skills and qualities:

- Visual perception
- Imagination
- Seeing what 'could be'
- Visual thinking
- Visual recall
- Parallel-parking a car
- Solving a jigsaw puzzle
- Daydreaming
- Creating new ideas in images
- Navigation
- Creating artwork/photographs/ video/painting/sculpture
- Assembling flat-pack furniture
- Map reading

> You don't take a photograph, you make it.
>
> *Ansel Adams*

...IN ACTION

To use and boost visual/spatial intelligence …

… provide these learning tools, and opportunities to use them:

- OHP and transparencies
- Camcorder and camera
- DVDs
- Mind maps
- Mind-mapping software
- Pens, pencils, paints
- Highlighter pens
- Artists' materials, tools and media
- Guided visualisation (someone talking you through images linked to learning, say a journey through the solar system, for you to imagine while they talk)
- Visual thinking tools (such as concept mapping)
- Diagrams
- Graphic novels, cartoon strips and comics
- Illustrated texts
- Infographics

… and suggest these careers:

- Film-maker
- Visual artist
- Navigator
- Film editor
- Production designer
- Photographer
- Cartographer
- Graphic designer
- Illustrator

Logical/mathematical intelligence

Nickname: **Logic Smart**

Area of the brain: **Pre-frontal cortex**

Your potential to think logically and to reason about the connections between objects, actions and ideas.

> Aerodynamically, the bumble bee shouldn't be able to fly, but the bumble bee doesn't know it, so it goes on flying anyway.
>
> *Mary Kay Ash*

Typical skills and qualities:

- Analysis
- Evaluation
- Reasoning
- Logical thought
- Winning debates/arguments
- Organising
- Planning
- Problem solving
- Scientific understanding
- Mathematical understanding
- Winning at Cluedo/Chess
- Developing strategies
- Getting out of trouble

> Your theory is crazy, but it's not crazy enough to be true.
>
> *Niels Bohr*

> No amount of experimentation can ever prove me right; a single experiment can prove me wrong.
>
> *Albert Einstein*

...IN ACTION

To use and boost logical/mathematical intelligence ...

... provide these learning tools, and opportunities to use them:

- Computers
- Calculators
- Measuring equipment
- Flow charts
- Logic problems
- Benjamin Bloom's Taxonomy*
- Edward De Bono's Six Thinking Hats†
- Ordered instructions
- *If ... then* statements
- Varied questions
- Venn diagrams
- The chance to challenge ideas

... and suggest these careers:

- Detective
- Cryptographer
- Scientist
- Mathematician
- Operations manager
- Politician
- Personal assistant
- Technician
- Lawyer
- IT analyst
- Engineer
- Researcher
- Computer programmer

* Bloom's Taxonomy classifies levels of thinking skills in learning.
† De Bono's Thinking Hats separates thinking into six categories, or roles, that learners adopt.

IDEA...

Verbal/linguistic intelligence

Nickname: **Word Smart**

Area of the brain: **Mainly left hemisphere**

Your potential to think in words and to understand how language is used effectively.

> The poet doesn't invent. He listens.
>
> *Jean Cocteau*

> A poet's work is to name the unnamable, to point at frauds, to take sides, start arguments, shape the world, and stop it going to sleep.
>
> *Salman Rushdie*

Typical skills and qualities:

- Reading
- Writing
- Speaking
- Listening
- Informing
- Describing
- Persuading
- Speaking more than one language
- Holding a conversation
- Mimicking verbally
- Telling jokes
- Leading
- Debating
- Writing or appreciating poetry

> Poetry is plucking at the heartstrings, and making music with them.
>
> *Dennis Gabor*

...IN ACTION

To use and boost verbal/linguistic intelligence …

… provide these learning tools, and opportunities to use them:

- Writing materials
- Dictionary
- Thesaurus
- Tape recorder and microphone
- Headphones
- Scripts
- Discussion time
- Books
- Word banks
- Audio recordings
- Songs
- The chance to ask questions

… and suggest these careers:

- Author
- Poet
- DJ/presenter
- Counsellor
- Negotiator
- Politician
- Help-desk operator
- Estate agent
- Lawyer

Interpersonal intelligence

Nickname: **People Smart**

Area of the brain: **Limbic system, pre-frontal cortex**

Your potential to think about other people and to understand the relationships you have with them.

> Fear makes strangers of people who would be friends.
>
> *Shirley Madame*

Typical skills and qualities:

- Teamwork
- Co-operation
- Collaboration
- Taking the lead
- Expressing emotions effectively
- Understanding others
- Persuading others
- Motivating others
- Recognising others' strengths
- Understanding human behaviour
- Negotiating
- Maintaining and growing relationships
- Managing others effectively
- Organising a party, event or excursion

> Friendship is a single soul dwelling in two bodies.
>
> *Aristotle*

> An insincere and evil friend is more to be feared than a wild beast; a wild beast may wound your body, but an evil friend will wound your mind.
>
> *Buddha*

...IN ACTION

To use and boost interpersonal intelligence…

… provide these learning tools, and opportunities to use them:

- Flexible seating/table arrangements
- Paired learning
- Genuine group work (collaboration)
- Teamwork (and so competition)
- Visits from experts
- Debates
- Discussions
- Interviews
- Community-building games
- Group presentations
- Teaching each other
- Assessing each other
- The chance to ask questions

… and suggest these careers:

- Teacher
- Office manager
- Help-desk operator
- Personal assistant
- Negotiator
- Estate agent
- Shop assistant
- Politician
- Life coach
- Events organiser
- Customer liaison officer
- Hair stylist
- Social worker
- Nurse

IDEA...

Intrapersonal intelligence

Nickname: **Self Smart**

Area of the brain: **Limbic system, pre-frontal cortex**

Your potential to think about yourself and to reflect on your thoughts, feelings and actions.

> He dares to be a fool, and that is the first step in the direction of wisdom.
>
> *James Gibbons Huneker*

Typical skills and qualities:

- Self-motivation
- Perseverance
- Self-knowledge
- Setting and meeting life goals
- Expressing emotions effectively
- Interest in how people think and behave
- Showing maverick tendencies
- Learning and working independently
- Following own interests
- Comfortable in own company
- Knowing own mind
- Dedication and loyalty
- Enterprising thoughts and actions
- Taking risks

> Remember, we all stumble, every one of us.
>
> *Emily Kimbrough*

> Patience is the companion of wisdom.
>
> *Saint Augustine*

...IN ACTION

To use and boost intrapersonal intelligence …

… provide these learning tools, and opportunities to use them:

- Flexible seating/table arrangements
- Individual learning
- Being the 'expert' in a group
- Space and time to reflect and think
- Visits from experts
- Text diaries
- Audio and video diaries
- Individual sets of resources
- Self-chosen study topics
- Individual presentations
- Target setting
- Self-assessment
- The chance to ask questions

… and suggest these careers:

- Explorer
- Teacher
- Inventor
- Athlete
- Parent
- Postman/woman
- Entrepreneur
- Writer
- Consultant
- Psychologist
- Pilot
- Artist

IDEA...

Bodily/kinesthetic intelligence

Nickname: **Body Smart/BK**

Area of the brain: **Sensory cortex, motor cortex**

Your potential to think in movements and to use your body.

> I've missed more than 9,000 shots in my career. I've lost almost 300 games. Twenty-six times, I've been trusted to take the game winning shot and missed. I've failed over and over and over again in my life. And that is why I succeed.
>
> *Michael Jordan*

> Acting is a matter of giving away secrets.
>
> *Ellen Barkln*

Typical skills and qualities:

- Fine motor skills (hands)
- Gross motor skills (body)
- Technical sport skills
- Technical artistic skills
- Acting
- Miming
- Dancing
- Gymnastics
- Building
- Construction
- Impersonation
- Role play
- Climbing
- Awareness of body

> It's good sportsmanship to not pick up lost golf balls while they are still rolling.
>
> *Mark Twain*

...IN ACTION

To use and boost bodily/kinesthetic intelligence …

… provide these learning tools, and opportunities to use them:

- Keyboard (both computer and musical)
- Construction kits
- Space to move around/change position
- Objects to handle
- Body language and hand gestures
- Writing materials
- Art materials
- Sports equipment
- Educational visits
- Hand signals and signs
- Kinesthetic assessment

… and suggest these careers:

- Sportsman/woman
- Dancer
- Artist
- Craftsperson
- Actor
- Factory worker
- Mechanic
- Stand-up comedian
- Sports coach
- Gardener
- Surgeon

IDEA...

Musical/rhythmic intelligence

Nickname:	**Music Smart**
Area of the brain:	**Right auditory cortex, limbic system**

Your potential to think in sounds and to understand how music is made, performed and appreciated.

> Music creates order out of chaos.
>
> *Yehudi Menuhin*

> Music was my refuge. I could crawl into the space between the notes and curl my back to loneliness.
>
> *Maya Angelou*

Typical skills and qualities:

- Sense of rhythm
- Singing
- Recalling the words of songs
- Technical skill with an instrument
- Dancing
- Writing songs
- Understanding music
- Making music
- Appreciating music
- Listening skills
- Being part of a band/group/orchestra
- Awareness of background music
- Humming while working
- Performing karaoke

> Music is the shorthand of emotion.
>
> *Leo Tolstoy*

...IN ACTION

To use and boost musical/rhythmic intelligence …

… provide these learning tools, and opportunities to use them:

- Music keyboard
- Drums
- Percussion instruments
- Opportunities to make music
- Music CDs
- Mp3 players
- Music software
- Background music
- Sound effects
- Music to express emotion
- Dance
- Concerts
- Performances

… and suggest these careers:

- Conductor
- DJ
- Record producer
- Session musician
- Singer
- Concert technician/roadie
- Singing teacher
- Voice coach
- Composer
- Radio producer
- Music teacher
- Choreographer
- Instrument maker/tuner
- Orchestra member

IDEA...

Naturalist intelligence

Nickname: **Nature Smart**

Area of the brain: **Not yet determined, but likely to involve the neural networks used in object recognition – visual areas towards the back of the brain**

Your potential to think about and understand the natural world.

Human subtlety will never devise an invention more beautiful, more simple or more direct than does Nature, because in her inventions, nothing is lacking and nothing is superfluous.

Leonardo Da Vinci

Typical skills and qualities:

- Recognising plants and animals
- Classifying plants and animals
- Understanding the natural world
- Caring for the environment
- Working and learning outside
- Appreciating natural history
- Organising information into hierarchies
- Organising information into taxonomies
- Caring for and spending time with pets
- Nurturing a garden
- Producing own fruit and veg
- Awareness of the natural world
- Astronomy
- Outdoor pursuits

Nature does nothing uselessly.

Aristotle

...IN ACTION

To use and boost naturalist intelligence …

… provide these learning tools, and opportunities to use them:

- Information presented in taxonomies
- Information presented in hierarchies
- Plants
- Space to work outdoors
- Animals
- CDs of nature sounds
- Educational visits and study trips
- Outdoor-adventure learning
- Orienteering-based challenges
- Scientific equipment
- Binoculars
- A window

… and suggest these careers:

- Farmer
- Marine biologist
- Vet
- Forest ranger
- Gardener
- Bee keeper
- Zoo keeper
- Explorer
- Conservationist
- Meteorologist
- Botanist
- Astronomer

Existential intelligence

Nickname: **Big-thinking Smart**

Area of the brain: **Temporal lobes and possibly integrating signals throughout the whole brain**

Your potential to think philosophically and to understand life, the universe and everything.

> Isn't it enough to see that a garden is beautiful without having to believe that there are fairies at the bottom of it too?
>
> *Douglas Adams*

Typical skills and qualities:

- Asking deep questions
- Understanding religion
- Thinking philosophically
- Interest in life beyond the Earth
- Seeking clarification and thorough understanding
- Comfortable not knowing … yet
- Contemplating

> I don't believe in God but I'm very interested in her.
>
> *Arthur C. Clarke*

So there you are – eight and a half different ways to value yourself and those you work with.

! But beware, for danger this way lies. Just as belief and expectation can limit and label people's intelligence, so too can an over-emphasis on one of the multiple intelligences. Thoughts, words and beliefs such as 'he's kinesthetic' or 'she's very linguistic' are helpful only for a while. They soon restrict learners to those skills. Far better to explore the full range of intelligences in each learner and get the big picture for them. The next chapter suggests how.

...IN ACTION

To use and boost existential intelligence ...

... provide these learning tools, and opportunities to use them:

- Challenging questions
- Space and time to think
- Space and time to work things out
- Provocative ideas
- Ethical debates
- Religious/philosophical points of view

... and suggest these careers:

- Religious leader
- Philosopher
- Healer
- Science-fiction author
- Counsellor
- Complementary therapist

IDEA...

Personalised learning

Personalised learning is the tailoring of teaching style, curriculum and learning contexts to meet the needs, aspirations and potential of individual learners.

Personalised learning is not a new concept. Schools have always tried to match teaching to children's needs. Personalised learning is a way to collect and share the best existing practice. There are five parts to it:

1. Assessment for learning
2. Effective teaching and learning
3. Curriculum entitlement and choice
4. School organisation
5. Strong partnership beyond the school.

Learn your learners!

A key aspect of personalised learning is understanding the person who is learning! The first step to individually tailored education, therefore, is knowing the person; knowing how they learn.

MI profiling

Multiple intelligences profiles provide quick and effective answers to the questions on the facing page.

In the following pages, there are five straightforward methods of devising multiple intelligences profiles.

In this chapter, discover how MI relates to personalised learning, find out about five ways to build up an MI profile, and see the consequences of MI for special needs and gifted learners.

...IN ACTION

Learning the person

Choose an individual learner whom you know fairly well. Answer these questions:

1. What are their unique skills?
2. What are their areas of weakness?
3. What is their potential?
4. How well do they know themselves – skills/weaknesses/potential?
5. What learning activities do they engage with best?
6. What careers would they suit?
7. What are their interests?

Learning the people

Now think about a group of learners – maybe a whole class – and ask yourself these questions:

1. Which learning activities do they engage with most?
2. In which areas do they generally excel?
3. In which areas do they generally need support?
4. How well do they know themselves – skills/weaknesses/potential?

Questionnaires

An MI questionnaire provides the opening credits to a dynamic film that tells the unique story of a learner's skills, talents, potential and achievements. It's a film that doesn't end. You never reach that definitive profile because learners continue to grow and change all their lives.

There are many formats for MI questionnaires. As well as the one on the facing page, you could try the two profile tools suggested below.

Before your learners begin filling in any, tell them the four golden rules of questionnaires:

1. This is not a test.
2. Answers are not right or wrong.
3. The results will confirm what you're good at and help to make your learning more effective.
4. Be true to yourself when you answer.

The MI wheel

This quick and easy profile from the Birmingham Grid for Learning has been completed by over 50,000 people.

Answer 40 preference-based questions online and your MI wheel appears: a pie chart of eight coloured sectors representing your combination of intelligences.

Find the wheel at: www.bgfl.org/multipleintelligences

MIDAS

Branton Shearer's MIDAS (Multiple Intelligences Developmental Assessment Scales) system has over 15 years' worldwide research and validation to its name. It breaks down each intelligence into three or four parts to provide a rich description of skills and potential. Versions are available for five different age groups.

Visit   www.thinkingclassroom.co.uk/ThinkingClassroom/MultipleIntelligences.aspx

...IN ACTION

Shade or half shade each check-box depending on how strongly you agree with each statement, to build a rough MI profile.

Verbal/ linguistic	I enjoy listening.
	I can talk my way out of trouble.
	I can persuade people to do things.
	I get/got into trouble for talking.
Logical/ mathematical	I can do maths easily.
	I spot mistakes easily.
	I am good at winning arguments.
	I like to plan ahead.
Visual/spatial	I have a good imagination.
	I am good at following maps.
	I like to draw/doodle.
	I get/got into trouble for daydreaming.
Bodily/ kinesthetic	I enjoy sport or physical activity.
	I like working with my hands.
	I get/got into trouble for not sitting still.
	I need to touch things to learn about them.
Musical/ rhythmic	I like singing or playing an instrument.
	I often listen to music.
	I know the songs in the chart.
	I hum or sing while playing or working.
Interpersonal	I know how I am feeling.
	I like working in a team.
	When I have a problem, I ask for help.
	I make friends easily.
Intrapersonal	I like working alone.
	I enjoy my own company.
	I know what I'm good at.
	When I have a problem, I sort it.
Naturalist	I enjoy spending time outside.
	I can name many plants/animals.
	I enjoy watching nature programmes.
	I enjoy caring for a pet/animals.
Existential	I go to a place of worship.
	I always ask why.
	I pray/meditate now and again.
	I believe in God.

Data

The world of education and learning is overloaded by numbers, levels, targets, statistics and performance data. It's a world that's data rich but may be information poor – not all of the figures provided are relevant, valuable and useful in practice.

Data can be used to track progress and to predict then provide the right levels of support for learners. It also highlights effective teaching and learning – if we choose to use the increase of a number to indicate this effectiveness.

However, data about achievements in learning is only beneficial if it is:

- Used to help learners to progress to the next stage in whatever the data is measuring.
- One of several assessment strategies – for example observation, self-assessment, peer review.
- Applied in order to motivate learners rather than to disengage and limit them.

> **TIP:**
> If you really must give someone a C grade, *do* celebrate it as an achievement, and then tell the learner how to get a B.

...IN ACTION

Turn data to your advantage by linking it to multiple intelligences and then building it into a learner's profile. For example:

- EYFS Profile information can be mapped onto most of the intelligences.
- End of Key Stage data can help to describe the linguistic, logical and naturalist intelligences.
- GCSE, and post-16 grades indicate strengths in various intelligence areas when the subject matches or partially matches an intelligence or intelligences.
- Day-to-day data (weekly test scores, for example) provides further pieces for the MI jigsaw.
- CAT (cognitive ability test) scores are used to indicate verbal and non-verbal intelligence and link to logical, visual and linguistic intelligences.

! Watch out though:

Data from a written exam or test is filtered by the linguistic intelligence: a learner's ability to show what they know will depend on how well they can read and write.

! And:

Some intelligences are not well represented out there in the world of data – how long might it be until we have a GCSE in emotional intelligence?

Observation

Observation of learners – their learning behaviour and the products of their learning – is something you'll do already as part of your assessment practice. But if you look again, this time informed by your knowledge of MI, what your learners do and say takes on a whole new significance.

Observations can be directed in several ways and it's advisable to keep them simple. Watching for signs of all intelligences in each learner every day is not recommended! You could focus on, for example:

- A single learner
- A group
- A specific subject linked to an intelligence
- Evidence of one intelligence
- A specific activity…

If you focus on a learner's …	Then you're looking at …
Response to and engagement with music	Musical intelligence
Reading and written work	Linguistic intelligence
Performance in group work and/or teamwork	Interpersonal intelligence
Independent working skills	Intrapersonal intelligence
Maths problem solving	Logical intelligence
Creation of artwork	Visual intelligence
Sports skills	Bodily intelligence
Interaction with the natural world	Naturalist intelligence
Depth of questioning	Existential (half) intelligence

...IN ACTION

When you spot the MI-related behaviour that you've chosen to look for, jot it down on a sticky note, with the date and learner's name.

> 26/5 Callum
> Moving in seat in time
> to music while
> watching Billy Elliot
> DVD - Musical? Bodily?

> 16/2 Kyra
> Went over to another
> pupil who was crying
> and cheered him up -
> Interpersonal.

> 6/1 Hassan
> Upset when Jade
> 'accidentally' moved his
> equipment out of the neat
> line he'd put it in -
> Logical? Naturalist?

It might be appropriate to share with other learners what you have seen and why you valued it. However, do be sensitive to individual preferences for public versus private compliments and comments.

File the observation notes in a folder – one sheet of paper for each learner. Overtime, mosaics of MI comments emerge, adding a valuable extra dimension to their MI profile.

Talking with parents

Parents are the world's experts on their own children, so why not tap into this well of knowledge and experience? You may not be able to meet with them regularly, and when you do time will probably be limited, but try to ask:

- What sort of person is your child?
- What do they enjoy doing?
- What are they good at?
- What do they avoid doing?
- What motivates them?
- What demotivates them?
- How do they choose to spend their free time?
- What do they dream of doing when they grow up?

These questions, or similar, could even be sent home for parents to reply to in writing. They could be used as preparation for, or prompts during, a meeting at parents' evening.

Involving parents further

Try to organise a parents' workshop aiming to:

- Introduce parents to the concept of multiple intelligences
- Kick-start an ongoing MI dialogue between parent, teacher and child
- Provide parents with the knowledge and vocabulary to talk about learning, skills and success.

Be sensitive to the starting point of your workshop audience: parents could well have more traditional ideas of intelligence, and there will be a range of views on what school should be like.

...IN ACTION

A parents' MI workshop could follow this format:

1. Welcome and thanks for coming
2. Rationale behind choosing to use MI
3. Introduction to each intelligence – refer to a famous person to exemplify each one
4. Parents fill out MI questionnaire (see page 35)
5. Share your old school reports and discuss how they match your strengths and weaknesses today
6. In small groups, parents share memories of school reports/experiences and discuss their MI profiles (from the questionnaire)
7. Explanation of how the school will be using MI
8. Explanation of how parents can help in profiling their children
9. Any questions.

Children could attend the workshop and fill out a questionnaire when parents do theirs. There's a lot of scope here for family interaction – looking at how intelligences do or don't get passed down generations or through family environments. But do be sensitive to family circumstances.

Talking with learners

Parents know their children well, but learners themselves have at least as valuable (self-) knowledge. Asking them to think about themselves as learners is an aspect of teaching and learning that is becoming more and more valued.

When they understand MI and know its vocabulary, learners will be able to assess MI in themselves. They'll probably know what they're good at already (though might need support in expressing it). MI provides a common language to describe individual strengths.

With your help, children can reflect on the results of their MI questionnaire, their experiences in school, their activities outside school and even consider whether they think their parents' views are accurate.

TIP:

The words chosen by learners might indicate intelligence strengths:

- I like the sound of that. (Musical/linguistic)
- That rings a bell. (Musical)
- I hear what you're saying. (Linguistic)
- I like the look of that. (Visual)
- Yes, I see what you mean. (Visual)
- I've got a good feeling about it. (Kinesthetic/existential/intrapersonal)
- One thing at a time. (Logical)

...IN ACTION

Below are several questions, in sections, to help learners reflect on their intelligences. You could use them in several ways:

- As a written assessment.
- Learners interviewing each other.
- Asked at the start of a year or course and again at the end; then results compared.
- Record responses from several learners as video or audio clips.

About learning

1. Which lessons do you most enjoy in school?
2. Which subjects do you do well at?
3. Which lessons do you least enjoy in school?
4. Which are your weakest subjects?

About free time

1. What do you do in your spare time?
2. What clubs/organisations are you involved in; which sports do you play?

About MI

1. Which intelligences are your strongest? How do you know this?
2. Is there a link between your strongest intelligences and what you do best – in and out of school?
3. What would your friends say are your strongest/weakest intelligences?
4. What would your teachers/parents say are your strongest/ weakest intelligences?

IDEA...

SEN, more able and G&T

A learner with a detailed MI profile no longer needs the option to be labelled as 'Special Needs' or 'Gifted', because the MI profile shows all areas of strength and weakness. What was previously a gift shows up as a peak on the profile; what used to be labelled a special need is now a dip in the profile.

This doesn't mean that specialist assessments for challenges such as dyslexia are any less valuable; in fact they help by feeding into the wider MI profile. A specialist dyslexia assessment provides very detailed information about verbal and non-verbal intelligences – which helps to guide the assessment of linguistic, logical and visual intelligences.

Remember that an MI profile is a powerful way to discover, value and use each learner's unique skills and talents for learning and it covers the full range of possible skills and talents.

Make use of the techniques suggested throughout this chapter to describe your learners, slowly and carefully, across the full range of human ability and potential rather than in a few narrow areas.

TIP:
Use the concept of multiple intelligences to see and better understand learning difficulties and learning differences.

...IN ACTION

In your organisation, listen out for comments such as:

We group them by ability.

She's special needs.

He's a gifted learner.

These phrases, and others like them, seem innocent enough, but try asking:

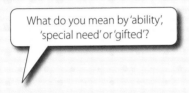

What do you mean by 'ability', 'special need' or 'gifted'?

You'll find that 'ability' often refers only to linguistic or mathematical ability.

'Special need', likewise, is deemed to be a weakness in linguistic, logical or behavioural skills. (Have you ever had to make provision for special musical or naturalist needs?)

A 'gifted' (or 'able' or 'talented') learner is said to be either a good all rounder (usually academic) or excelling in one or two skill areas.

Gently and respectfully challenge the use of systems that label learners by a narrow set of criteria.

Walls

The organisation of display space provides a highly visible and easily sustainable opportunity to describe, value and use the different intelligences.

Labels

Raise the profile of MI without having to move or buy anything: label the areas of your teaching space that already demonstrate one or more intelligences (see facing page).

If you are restricted to a science lab or any other subject-specific space, work with what you have. Look through an MI lens and label as much as you can, for example microscopes as *Visual;* science text books as *Linguistic.*

Posters

Put up posters of celebrities and other successful people. Annotate the posters with the intelligences the people have used to succeed.

Affirmations

Affirmations are first-person present-tense positive statements of aspiration and achievement that should be read or said regularly (see facing page). They fill your mind with optimistic thoughts, preventing negative ones from getting a foothold.

Your teaching space might be the classroom where you spend the whole year, or a conference room used for a day. You may have total or almost no influence on how this area is arranged, but if you can, infuse MI into your surroundings. Give your teaching space an intelligent makeover.

...IN ACTION

Label the book corner (or equivalent) and listening station: **Linguistic area**.

Set aside spaces with individual seating, naming them: **Intrapersonal areas**.

Label an art space: **Bodily and Visual area**.

Get your learners to represent the following affirmations in an artistic medium or particular style of their choice:

> I am intelligent. I am valuable. I succeed.
>
> I have unique skills and talents.
>
> I am becoming more intelligent.

Encourage learners to create and represent, in their own way, their own affirmation.

Display posters that describe the intelligences. You could download a set for free from www.thinkingclassroom.co.uk.

As a homework task, challenge your learners to profile a famous person. Ask them to include a picture and their strongest intelligences. Collect these into a classroom display. Examples are:

Richard Branson – Interpersonal; Intrapersonal; Logical
Ellen MacArthur – Intrapersonal; Naturalist; Bodily
Gandhi – Existential; Interpersonal; Linguistic
Robbie Williams – Musical; Interpersonal; Intrapersonal
Dakota Fanning – Linguistic; Intrapersonal
George Lucas – Visual; Linguistic; Interpersonal

Furniture and resources

The layout plan opposite demonstrates how a classroom can be organised for MI.

As with all the ideas in this chapter, pick and choose what will work for you and your learners.

The floor plan is an example of how some of the MI environment suggestions can be brought together in a primary classroom. Aspects of this approach can be adapted for use in specialist secondary classrooms.

There are no particular reasons for specific placement of the MI areas or resources, the layout is simply a demonstration that everything *can* be included.

...IN ACTION

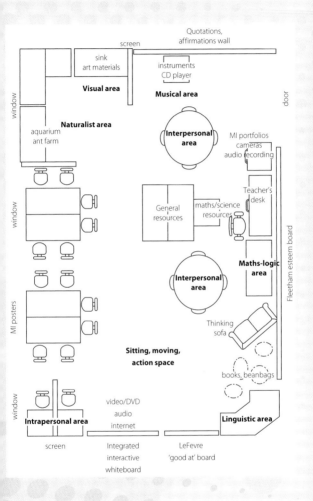

Fleetham esteem boards

If you can, set aside about 75 per cent of your available display space for a Fleetham esteem board. It's an effective way to:

- Publicly value your learners
- Track their progress
- Celebrate their achievements
- Have a quick reference of their preferences and strengths.

The board can work in a variety of ways and places – in a classroom, tutor room or corridor. Adapt it to your own needs and circumstances.

...IN ACTION

1. Divide the display board area into a grid – one 'cell' for each learner. Include yourself and any adults with whom you teach.
2. Set up each cell, with your learners' help, to include:
   - A named photograph or portrait.
   - A self-chosen, annotated piece of work.
   - An MI profile bar chart (see below).
3. Transfer the information from first-draft MI profiles onto bar charts. Mark blocks on each learner's chart:
   - Colour in one block for each intelligence.
   - Colour in two extra blocks on each of the learner's two strongest intelligences.
   - Colour in one extra block on each of the next two strongest intelligences.

Linguistic										
Logical										
Musical										
Visual										
Kinesthetic										
Interpersonal										
Intrapersonal										
Naturalist										
Existential										

4. Every so often, ask learners to replace their annotated work. Place the removed pieces in learners' portfolios.
5. Three times a year, add more blocks to the charts to show how learners are developing. Your ongoing profiling will indicate where new blocks should go.
6. Attach sticky notes that record significant MI advances.

! A note on adding blocks

Colouring in additional blocks is more art than science. It's best to set aside some time to review the MI–related information that you've gathered (see Chapter 3). Then judge if and when a learner has become more intelligent.

Words, thoughts, beliefs

What you say comes from what you think; what you think comes from what you believe. Therefore, your words reveal your beliefs.

Your teaching space and time will be enriched if you model and encourage the use of MI language:

> In PE today, our challenge is to improve our ball skills and tactics; so we're going to need our BK (bodily/kinesthetic) intelligence and what else?

> Your challenge is to create a map of our local area 70 years ago. Which intelligences will we need to do this?

> Your linguistic intelligence needs to come into play during German lessons.

> Great! That's an effective sentence, good use of your linguistic intelligence.

> Why do we need to use our logical and visual intelligences in maths today?

! Beware:

The language and implicit beliefs of multiple intelligences can be confusing and threatening to some learners. Their identity, security and safety might come from a sense of not being clever. They may (very cleverly in fact) construct a belief that 'acting stupid' makes life easier and helps them to avoid hard work. Respect where learners such as this are coming from and persevere patiently. They will come round.

...IN ACTION

Do try to use 'intelligent' and its various synonyms as often as you can:

MI language

When you use MI language, your learners will begin to use it too. They'll have a vocabulary for expressing success and one for discussing learning. You might find that their development of MI language follows a pattern similar to the stages below.

Stage 1: The learner's excuse

A short while after you introduce MI, a learner might use it as an excuse:

Teacher: Please stand still outside Mr M's office.
Learner: I can't because I'm BK.

Stage 2: The parent's excuse

Then parents use MI as an excuse for their children:

Parent: He's linguistic you know, so he's going to talk in class.

This stage is encouraging, however, because it indicates that students have spoken to their parents about MI.

Stage 3: Spontaneous use

Next, learners use MI language independently:

Teacher: So why do you want to be a film editor?
Learner: Well I reckon I could use my visual and interpersonal intelligences.

Stage 4: Creative use

Finally, some learners begin to work out the intelligence profiles of their friends, relatives and even pets:

Learner: I reckon I know the intelligences of all my family and my baby brother too. My cat's BK, visual and interpersonal and naturalist.
Teacher: How did you work that out?
Learner: Because he catches birds and plays around with them.

...IN ACTION

Listen out for MI language and record it as evidence that your learners are beginning to understand the concept. Scribble on sticky notes, use a tape recorder, a laptop, a video camera; and ask your teaching assistant to listen out for MI vocabulary too.

Do reflect your observations back to your learners – share the notes, play the tapes – this demonstrates that you value their use of these specific words and phrases.

If you find a learner using MI as an excuse, use the language of MI to rebut the excuse:

Please stand still outside Mr M's office.

I can't because I'm BK.

If you're BK, you should be able to control your body.

ENRICH YOUR TEACHING

IDEA...

Planning

What range of activities do you provide for your learners? Do they get to:

- Read from textbooks?
- Talk to each other?
- Work in collaborative groups?
- Copy from a book or board?
- Listen to you and each other?
- Make video presentations?
- Follow their own interests?
- Create artwork?
- Ask difficult questions?
- Follow instructions?
- Try a mix of the above and more?

There's a good chance you'll set up learning experiences based on your own intelligences strengths – and why not? That's what you do best.

But what about those students with other intelligences? Should they be expected to adapt to your style or should you bend to theirs …?

There's no need to completely rewrite your planning to take account of multiple intelligences. Whether your planning is subject–based, short, medium or long term, or the whole curriculum, you can easily enrich it.

This section suggests how to introduce and integrate simple, effective MI teaching activities and resources. You can apply MI ideas to enhance the work that you do already.

...IN ACTION

1. Examine a piece of planning (such as the short-term example below) through an 'MI lens' – how is MI already incorporated, even if not yet by name?
2. Next, decide how you want to move forward with MI ideas – will you change or add activities? Alter language and questioning? Introduce MI explicitly?
3. Finally, pencil in changes, see how they go, and then note down what, if anything, you'll change next time.

Before

Learning objective	Activity
Be able to enhance a piece of writing by researching and selecting alternative adjectives	• Working in pairs, highlight adjectives from p39 of *The Amber Spyglass* • Select 5 adjectives, look up alternatives in thesaurus • Select alternative adjectives • Share results with another pair

After

Learning objective	Activity
Be able to enhance a piece of writing by researching and selecting alternative adjectives *Linguistic focus/ Naturalist with thesaurus?/ Interpersonal?*	• Working in pairs, highlight adjectives from p39 of *The Amber Spyglass* *Give choice of working alone, give choice of non-fiction text – own choice?* • Select 5 adjectives, look up alternatives in thesaurus • Select alternative adjectives • Share results with another pair *Offer choices to: score word choices out of 10 (M/L); read enriched text to group (Ling); find material to illustrate adjectives (Vis). Ask how they could use skills learned.*

57

Assessment

While summative assessment sums up what's been achieved so far, *formative* assessment informs the next steps of learning.

Most assessment favours linguistic and logical intelligences, but there are ways to work alongside this system *and* value the varied intelligences of your learners.

One of the keys to successful *formative* assessment is to involve learners in the process. Let learners use what they're good at to show what they know and what they can do. There are many ways for learners to demonstrate, for example, their grasp of adjectives:

Intelligence	Example of assessed product
Musical	Write and perform a song or jingle including specific adjectives
Linguistic	Rewrite a piece of text with alternative adjectives
Naturalist	Classify adjectives into some form of hierarchy, such as colours, sounds, textures
Interpersonal	Collaborate with one or more people to make products like those in this table
Intrapersonal	Prepare a diary (own or on behalf of historical/scientific/other character) which includes descriptive adjectives. Describe self
Visual	Choose appropriate media, style and form to convey meanings of adjectives through artwork
Mathematical	Sort adjectives into a 2- or 3-ring Venn diagram – criteria such as 'can describe a river'/'can describe a mountain'/'both'
Bodily	Plan and perform a dance, role play, mime or frieze to communicate meanings

...IN ACTION

Writing is often favoured as a form of assessment because it provides a permanent record. Technology now offers alternative ways to find equally enduring evidence.

Allow learners to choose one or more of the following to demonstrate their knowledge and skills:

- Digital photographs
- Video clips
- Web pages
- Audio clips
- Slide-show presentations (such as PowerPoint)
- CD/DVD portfolios
- Online portfolios
- Documents and files on word processor
- Spreadsheets
- Campus radio programmes
- Music software
- Video software
- Art software
- Mind-mapping software.

At the end of a learning experience, ask perceptive and challenging MI questions about both the product and process. Encourage learners to ask these questions of each other and to feed their answers into the next activity:

- What did you find most difficult?
- What did you find easiest?
- Which intelligences did you use?
- Would other intelligences have helped?
- Have you become cleverer during this activity?
- What will you try to do next time?
- Are there any skills you need to work on?

MI teaching ideas – starters

You only get one chance to start a lesson. How you do it can make or break the success of whatever else you've planned for that time.

Lesson starters need to be:

- Engaging
- Inspiring
- Relevant to previous learning
- Linked to and leading into the main part of the session
- Delivered with the plenary session in mind.

(Well, most of the above – you don't want to burn out too quickly!)

Variety is important in lesson introductions, otherwise you come to sound like the front man of a support act at a concert: '… and here's another one off the latest album …'

The use of multiple intelligences offers variety if, over time, you let different intelligences guide your starting activities.

The 15 suggestions on the facing page are a variety of ways, grouped by intelligence, to kick off the same geography lesson on types of settlement.

...IN ACTION

Logical

Pose higher-order questions:

1. What if city growth was not limited?
2. Which is better – village or hamlet?
3. Which is the odd one out: city, conurbation, town, village?
4. If 'Pollution' is the answer, what is the question?
5. I wonder why people like living in cities …?

Linguistic

6. Solve these anagrams: iyct, gilavle, ethlam, wton.
7. Tell the person next to you five positive things about living in a city.
8. Play two short audio clips: one recorded in a city centre, the other recorded in a village centre – both 11am on Saturday morning.
9. Read an extract from a relevant text for learners to keep a mental tally of how often a keyword appears ('city', for example).

Visual

10. One slice at a time, reveal more of a photograph of a settlement (covered initially by a piece of card), each time giving learners the chance to predict what is still hidden.
11. Play games of odd one out with different photographs of villages, cities and so on.
12. Using the audio tapes in Linguistic above, visualise where the recordings were made.
13. Give learners 60 seconds to sketch an image that represents 'city' or 'village'.

Bodily

14. Handle a variety of objects and predict the places they have travelled through –for example: newspaper (city printers, city warehouse, van, village newsagent, home), toy car, carrier bag, button, plastic drinking glass.
15. Get learners to line up according to how much they like where they live (the place, not their homes): Love it' at one end, 'Hate it' at the other, 'Not fussed' in the centre.

IDEA...

MI teaching ideas – literacy

The teaching of literacy is a very good place to start trying out MI learning activities. There are several reasons for this:

1. Language links easily to all MI areas. It is used extensively to express and assess all curriculum subjects and therefore the areas of multiple intelligences appearing in those subjects. For example, some aspects of PE are taught through listening and reading and they are assessed through writing.
2. Effective communication is a prerequisite for success in life, work and learning.
3. Education is language-based.

The approach is *not* a case of:

Let's do MI instead of just reading and writing.

A more helpful and practical view is:

Let's use MI to improve the teaching and learning of literacy.

TIP:
Notice that learners' book choices will indicate their intelligence strengths and confirm the shape of their profiles.

...IN ACTION

Enhancing the experience of text

Intell.	Enhancement activity
V/L	<ul><li>Listen for and tally keywords.</li><li>Write down certain types of word, e.g. 3-letter/verbs/adjectives.</li><li>Two groups read a sentence or line alternately.</li></ul>
L/M	<ul><li>Perform a word/letter count.</li><li>Use a Venn diagram to represent one aspect of the text.</li><li>Make a flow chart of the plot.</li></ul>
M/R	<ul><li>Add a soundtrack – music or sounds that support the text.</li><li>Emphasise the rhythm in the text.</li><li>Model and encourage intonation.</li></ul>
V/S	<ul><li>Provide images or objects to support the meaning.</li><li>Create a mind map of the meaning.</li><li>Close eyes and visualise the meaning.</li></ul>
Inter	<ul><li>Paired discussion about a specific aspect of the text.</li><li>Emphasise emotions in the text.</li><li>Read the text all together in sync.</li></ul>
Intra	<ul><li>Use individual copies of the text.</li><li>Give time to reflect on the text.</li><li>Write personal response.</li></ul>
B/K	<ul><li>Use finger movements and sounds to punctuate the text.</li><li>Move hands up and down to indicate intonation or theme.</li><li>Illustrate the text with human tableaux.</li></ul>
E	<ul><li>Explore deeper meanings – ask 'Why?', 'How?' and 'What does this say about life?'.</li><li>Give thinking and pondering time.</li></ul>
N	<ul><li>Relate the text to nature.</li><li>Organise the words into a hierarchy: top layer – all words; next layer – verbs/nouns/adjectives/adverbs …</li><li>Read in a different place from normal.</li></ul>

MI teaching ideas – spelling and punctuation

Multiple intelligences can be used in every area of communication – from reading, writing, debating, persuading and so on, to the sub-skills needed for these things to happen effectively. Although spelling and punctuation are about as linguistic as you can get, the teaching of them lends itself readily to alternative, MI-inspired activities.

On the opposite page you'll see a couple of ideas on how to use MI in literacy 'basics', but don't feel restricted by my suggestions. Feel free to create your own actions and sounds to represent not only punctuation marks but other signs and symbols that are regularly encountered. Involve your learners too – they will come up with some great ideas. Consider how, for example, you could represent 'Line up quietly, please' with an action and a sound.

Likewise, each intelligence provides many many ways to experience and learn high-frequency words and keywords. Build on the examples given. A ten-minute brainstorming sessions with colleagues could yield well over 30 ideas (a class of nine-year-olds I once taught came up with 55!).

...IN ACTION

Finger punctuation

Teach your learners the following finger or hand air actions to illustrate different punctuation marks in a text.

Punctuation mark	Action
.	Poke
?	Draw a question mark (finishing with a poke)
!	Draw a straight line down, plus poke
' '	Two fingers make rabbit ears
,	Flick down with finger
/	Karate chop
( )	Both hands make brackets
...	Three pokes
;	Finger and thumb poke, then thumb flick
:	Finger and thumb poke together

MI spelling

Here is one task for each intelligence to support the learning and recall of new vocabulary:

- **Musical:** Record words and play them back.
- **Verbal:** Make a sentence including all new vocabulary.
- **Interpersonal:** Play charades.
- **Intrapersonal:** Set own targets.
- **Visual:** Put the words on cards on a tray – look at them, cover them, remove one – which has gone?
- **Logical:** Invent anagrams.
- **Bodily:** Finger-write words in sand or in condensation on a window.
- **Naturalist:** Organise words into a hierarchy of interest, importance, usefulness, ease of learning, or any other relevant categories.

MI and ICT

The vast and expanding world of information technology provides all sorts of opportunities to use different intelligences for learning.

Learners will very often engage more readily with material if it appears on a computer screen than if it is placed in front of them on a printed page. The tools of ICT allow subject content to be presented and assessed in many new and appealing ways – ways that play to learners' strengths. For example, the water cycle can be viewed and interacted with as an online animation (just search the internet!), and learners can then easily create their own audio-visual presentations about it using slide-show and animation software such as Microsoft *PowerPoint*.

The speed of technological change can at times seem overwhelming and expensive, but the latest gadgets, devices and computer programs are gradually becoming easier to use, and often cheaper. Once we've mastered one internet browser, digital camera or Mp3 player, the latest upgrade is usually straightforward to operate and offers even greater learning experiences.

The following ideas are adapted from *New Tools for Learning* by John Davitt (Network Continuum Education), a book that makes practical sense of the vastness of ICT on offer, and gives you a map for the expansion of your own resources.

...IN ACTION

Look through this table and choose three tools and three tasks that you could provide for your learners. Build them into your planning for next term.

Intell.	Tools	Tasks
V/L	• Email • Audio-editing software • Speaking word processors	• Radio show/podcast • Communication across the globe
L/M	• Spreadsheet • Control-language software (Logo) • Web design/editing	• Collect/process data • Enhance web page
M/R	• Keyboards • Sound files • Music production software	• Soundtracks for performance • Sound effects for a story/play
V/S	• Scanner • Animation software • Digital camera	• Ten-photo animation • Animation to explain an idea
Inter	• Discussion/message boards • Video conferencing • Camcorder	• Collaboration with other organizations • Interviews • Sound bites and vox pops
Intra	• Website • Mp3 files	• Online autobiography • Learning diary
B/K	• Dance mat • Touch screen • Webcam for interacting with games consoles (such as iToy)	• Clay animation • Large screen video projection
N	• Sound recorder • Environmental sensors • Satellite navigation system	• Multimedia field study • Weather monitoring and forecasting

Being an MI teacher

Teachers who have begun to think, work and learn with multiple intelligences show several distinguishing characteristics. They:

- Believe that all learners are intelligent.
- Believe that the level of each intelligence can increase.
- Have a good understanding of MI theory.
- Make use of MI concepts to identify and nurture specific talents in their learners.
- Use stronger intelligences to support and develop weaker ones.
- Give learners choices of activity.
- Use MI to model real-world problem solving.
- Know their learners' intelligences profiles.
- Know how MI relates to their curriculum.
- Can and do provide activities for most if not all intelligences.
- Encourage learner self-reflection.
- Assess in ways other than just linguistic.
- Show a willingness to try something new.

...IN ACTION

Pick one method of teaching that you've never tried before!
Give it a go and see how your learners respond. If possible,
choose something that matches the learners' needs.

Intell.	Teaching technique
V/L	• Encourage persuasion and debate. • Tell stories. • Share your linguistic talents and interests.
L/M	• Reason, enquire, evaluate and analyse. • Explain the steps of a lesson at the start. • Share your logical talents and interests.
M/R	• Incorporate sound, voice and music. • Encourage composition and appreciation of music. • Share your musical talents and interests.
V/S	• Look and watch – videos, photographs, diagrams. • Use mind maps. • Share your visual talents and interests.
Inter	• Encourage collaborative group work. • Show interest in learners' lives. • Share aspects of your life outside school.
Intra	• Encourage independent work. • Reflect on, audit and develop your teaching and learning. • Share some of your thoughts and feelings.
B/K	• Provide opportunities to move and handle. • Explain concepts with hand movements. • Share your bodily talents and interests.
N	• Draw attention to the natural world. • Use hierarchies and taxonomies. • Share naturalist talents and interests.
E	• Encourage 'Why?' and 'How?' questions. • Encourage extended thinking. • Share your existential talents and interests.

IDEA...

MI and thinking skills

Thinking skills are the conscious mental processes that we use to gather, manage, store and retrieve information.

The many skills of thinking have been categorised in over 50 different ways, but researchers at Newcastle University have done a great job summarising them into a simple model:

Strategic/reflective thinking skills

Cognitive thinking skills
- Information gathering
- Basic understanding
- Productive thinking

Cognitive thinking

Information-gathering skills include:
- Sensing – seeing, hearing, touching
- Retrieving – memory skills.

Basic understanding skills include:
- Organising gathered information
- Forming concepts
- Linking ideas together.

Productive thinking skills include:
- Using gathered information and basic understanding
- Applying, solving problems, making decisions, creating, analysing, evaluating.

Strategic and reflective thinking

This is thinking about thinking – planning, monitoring and evaluating your use of the cognitive skills above.

Here you can discover the relationship between MI, thinking skills and learning styles and see practical ways to combine them in your teaching and learning, and then apply these ideas to problem solving and creative thinking.

...IN ACTION

Learners will find an activity more engaging if a combination of thinking skills and intelligences are on offer. When you choose or design experiences, include:

- Information gathering
- Basic understanding
- Productive thinking
- Strategic/reflective thinking
- At least three intelligences.

To make it easier to design activities, ask yourself:

- What information do the learners need to have and how will they get it?
- How will learners relate new information to what they already know?
- How will learners use what they learn?
- What will learners make or do to show that they have learned?
- How will learners reflect on and evaluate their thinking and learning?

Designing like this is easy and you probably do it already. Here's a straightforward example that summarises the idea.

- **Watch:** A video about Hitler's invasion of Poland.
- **Discuss:** Key events with a partner.
- **Consider:** Did anyone try to stop Hitler?
- **Think:** How would you attempt to influence a decision by your own government?
- **Make:** A script, audio and/or visual slogan in the style of WWII propaganda for a chosen 21st–century issue.
- **Think:** What has been learned? What skills were developed? What next?

MI and learning styles

Learning styles are our unique and preferred ways to experience new information. Often confused with multiple intelligences, learning styles describe the 'front end' of learning; whereas the intelligences are more (but not exclusively) to do with showing what we *have* learned, at the other end.

A model developed by Barbara Prashnig (founder of *Creative Learning Systems*) shows just how much there is to learning styles.

She considers all the factors that play a part in a learner's ability to handle new and/or difficult information. Here are the six different areas of preference she lists, with illustrative examples:

Brain wiring
Do you think analytically or holistically?

Senses
Do you prefer to see, hear, touch, move …?

Physical
Early morning or late at night?

Environment
Comfortable or formal? Bright light or dim?

Social
With friends or alone? Authority or not?

Attitude
Are you self-motivated? Do you conform?

...IN ACTION

For an even richer learning experience, bring learning styles into the teaching equation, along with multiple intelligences. Although they are not separate concepts, they *are* distinct ways of thinking about the design of learning experiences.

Because of their different intelligences, learners have unique skills with which they demonstrate what they know. Some of these skills can also be used to experience new and/or difficult information, thus making use of learning styles.

- Suggest to learners with a strong bodily/kinesthetic intelligence that they can experience new information by touching and moving.
- Suggest to learners with a strong visual/spatial intelligence that they can experience new information by watching and visualising.
- Suggest to learners with a strong interpersonal intelligence that they can experience new information by learning collaboratively.

MI and problem solving

> Too many problem-solving sessions become battlegrounds where decisions are made based on power rather than intelligence.
>
> *Margaret J. Wheatley*

What was the last problem you faced?

- A difficult student/colleague
- A subject-based question
- You've run out of ideas
- Lack of energy
- Stress
- Debt
- Relationship/family

Have you dealt with it, or is it still an issue?

Sometimes you need outside help; sometimes you need time to sort it out; sometimes the problem simply disappears without you having to act.

You and your learners will have different methods for solving problems and MI can be part of your repertoire. MI is powerful because each intelligence is a starting point for possible solutions.

You can use MI problem solving with your learners in a couple of ways: to directly address their problems, concerns and issues (see right) and to gain a deeper and wider grasp of subject content.

...IN ACTION

Let's say you're feeling more stress than you're comfortable with. **STOP.** Take a minute to list some ways to relax.

Now write the list again, but use each intelligence as a prompt. This time, you might end up with:

Musical	Intrapersonal
<ul><li>Listen to relaxation music.</li><li>Sing favourite song.</li><li>Learn to play drums.</li></ul>	<ul><li>Examine feelings.</li><li>Record your feelings.</li><li>Set personal limits on stress.</li></ul>
Linguistic	**Visual**
<ul><li>Get lost in a book.</li><li>Talk things over with a friend.</li><li>Listen to favourite comedian.</li></ul>	<ul><li>Go to the cinema.</li><li>Watch TV or a DVD.</li><li>Take up some form of art.</li></ul>
Existential	**Mathematical**
<ul><li>Visit a holy place.</li><li>Meditate/pray.</li><li>Ask: 'How big is your stress on a world scale?'</li></ul>	<ul><li>Analyse the stress – ask why/who/how.</li><li>Create a plan for dealing with it.</li><li>Do puzzles such as sudoku.</li></ul>
Naturalist	**Bodily**
<ul><li>Go for a walk.</li><li>Make fuss of a pet.</li><li>Sort CDs/books by A–Z or theme.</li></ul>	<ul><li>Run/swim/play sport.</li><li>Take a long bath or shower.</li><li>Have a massage.</li></ul>
Interpersonal	
<ul><li>Have a night out with friends.</li><li>Find out how other people deal with stress.</li><li>See a counsellor.</li></ul>	

IDEA...

Creative problem solving

Here are several starting points for MI creative problem solving. The scenarios indicate how time spent finding solutions is time spent learning curriculum content.

Subject	Problem to solve in eight different ways
Food technology	A leisure group has asked you to come up with original ideas for a new themed restaurant. What could you create?
A&D	You are a successful but bored painter. What new art forms or techniques could you turn your hand to?
PSHE	Two friends have just been moved on from the town centre by the police. How can they occupy their time legally and responsibly, and have fun and be creative too?
D&T	A wealthy inventor has invited you to construct any machine you like. What would you propose to her?
Geography	Inner-city overcrowding is straining services and resources. What can be done?
English	An author is suffering from writer's block. He needs ideas for his next book.
MFL	You are stuck in a country abroad, and you don't know the language. How could you go about learning it?
Drama	An actor has started to forget her lines. How could she remember them?
Dance	You have to perform a dance to an audience of 1,000 people who don't like dance. What can you do?

...IN ACTION

Here are some possible responses to the first scenario (setting up a themed restaurant) that draw on different intelligences.

Look out for something similar when challenging your learners with the problem. Or, if they are struggling at the start of the activity but you know their MI profiles, offer these ideas as prompts to get their creative ideas flowing.

Real-life learning

Expert MI researchers Julie Viens, Susan Baum and Barbara Slatin have discovered many many ways that educators use MI. They call one category of approaches the Authentic Problems Pathway (one of five 'pathways' that they found).

This is an engaging approach for learners because it:

- Involves real projects with real timescales and products
- Casts them in genuine team/expert roles
- Provides opportunities for authentic assessment of learning (rather than being staged like an exam)
- Lets them use a wide range of intelligences
- Gives them a chance to apply their learning
- Allows them to work independently of you.

! Beware:

Learners will need certain skills before they attempt a real-life learning project. If they will be working in a group, for example, they need some experience of:

- Taking turns
- Supporting colleagues
- Sharing an aim
- Accepting responsibility
- Assuming a role.

And if they are to communicate effectively, learners need to:

- Speak clearly
- Listen
- Ask questions.

Creating real-life projects and developing collaborative work are well worth the effort. You prepare your learners for the world while teaching them skills, subject matter and attitudes.

Find out more about this approach at:
www.thinkingclassroom.co.uk

...IN ACTION

Set up collaborative MI groups and provide realistic projects directly linked to subject content.

Groups and teams can be much more effective when each member has a specific responsibility. MI strengths can be encouraged as follows:

Timekeeper

- Use your logical/mathematical skills.
- When does the task need to be finished? How much time do you have?
- How will you let the group know how long is left?

Facilitator

- Use your interpersonal skills.
- Does every team member have something to do?
- Has everyone had a say? How is everyone feeling?
- Is the team doing what it's supposed to?

Image consultant

- Use your visual/spatial skills.
- What information do you need to present? How can this be done clearly?
- What colours/style/design will suit the information?

Communication expert

- Use your verbal/linguistic skills.
- What needs writing and saying?
- What form does the writing/speaking take?
- What are the needs of the audience?

IT analyst

- Use your logical/mathematical skills.
- What software features should be used?
- Do you have the necessary equipment?
- How will you work with other group members?

MI and creativity

Creativity in learning is more than using art or poetry to learn key facts. It's about using imagination to make things that haven't been made before and do things that haven't been done before. Creativity means taking a risk to try out different ways of teaching and learning.

Creative MI moments

Some of our best ideas come to us with little effort and when we least expect them. In fact, the harder we try to have sparky new ideas or to think up ingenious solutions, the more elusive they become. But there are times and places when creative thoughts sneak up unaware: in the shower; just before sleep; as you wake up; while running, swimming or driving …

MI can recognise your own creative moments, and suggest new ones to try:

Intelligence	While …
Musical	Listening to music, singing
Linguistic	Deep in conversation
Existential	Meditating; praying
Naturalist	Walking in the city or countryside
Interpersonal	Working with others, socialising
Intrapersonal	Alone; reflecting; sleeping
Visual	Daydreaming; in guided meditation
Mathematical	Facing a problem
Bodily	Showering; exercising

Ask your learners when and where they have their best ideas and then offer them a range of experiences to stimulate creative moments.

...IN ACTION

MI creative matrix

By selecting one item from each column, you automatically create a possible teaching and learning experience. Not all of them will work or even make sense, but there are 512 possibilities here (8×8×8)!, and many of them will be new, interesting and effective.

MI-inspired product	Organisation of learning	Curriculum content
Song to the tune of 'Good King Wenceslas' (Musical)	Whole class	Using weekly spellings
Interview (Linguistic)	Small groups	Applying number facts
Taxonomy or hierarchy (Naturalist)	One-to-one	Learning classroom rules
Collaborative group presentation (Interpersonal)	ICT suite	Recounting a historical event
Learning diary (Intrapersonal)	Peer coaching	Defining product requirements
Set of digital photographs (Visual)	Circle time	Learning subject keywords
Flow chart (Logical)	Trip around school grounds	Exploring religious beliefs
Clay model (Kinesthetic)	Homework	Designing a science experiment

In small groups, recount a historical event through a series of digital photographs.

A development programme

You might pick out ideas from this book every now and again, but if you want to infuse MI into your whole organisation, some form of development plan is in order. Here's a suggestion from Howard Gardner:

Six key stages for MI implementation

1. Learn more about MI theory and practices.
2. Form study groups.
3. Visit institutions that are incorporating MI ideas.
4. Attend conferences that feature MI ideas.
5. Join a network of similar organisations that are exploring and using MI ideas. Include those in different countries if at all possible.
6. Plan and launch activities, practices or programmes that grow out of immersion in the world of MI theory and approaches.

The opposite page demonstrates how it might work for you.

...IN ACTION

Step 1 – Preparation

- Establish a rationale for using MI to enrich teaching and learning.
- Make a personal commitment to using MI in your organisation.
- Choose an MI text, read it and get a copy for each member of staff.

Step 2 – Team meeting 1 (1 hour)

- Explain the rationale and reasons for committing to MI.
- Present a brief summary of MI theory and practice.
- Distribute books and allocate sections or chapters to small groups.
- Give groups the next session and the remainder of this one to read their section and prepare an activity to teach to everyone else – the activity must reflect one or more of the intelligences.

Step 3 – Team meeting 2 (1 hour)

- Reading and activity preparation time.

Step 4 – Team meeting 3 (1–2 hours)

- Small groups teach their section of the book, using an MI–inspired activity.
- After each activity, groups feed back their understanding to the whole group.

Step 5 – Team meeting 4 (1 hour)

- Develop MI action plans linked to new-found understanding, integrated with existing improvement plans.

Step 6 – Implementation and review

- Carry out actions, monitor and feed back to team. Celebrate and adjust ideas as necessary.

Supporting educational transition

There is a well-known dip in academic performance as learners move from one stage of education to another. In the UK this is particularly noticeable when going from infant to junior and primary to secondary education. Dropout rates in further education are high, and learners going back into education or taking up training often find the experience a challenge. So much is changing around learners that learning often ends up taking a back seat.

Professor Maurice Galton has identified five 'bridges' that learners have to cross during this transition:

Administrative
  Different paperwork/systems

Social/emotional
  Friends, feelings, fears

Curriculum
  New subjects, new things to learn

Pedagogy
  Different ways of being taught

Management of learning
  Different ways to learn

Each bridge presents challenges, but Galton argues that support for learners has often been wrongly focused on only the first two rather than all five. However, he also stresses that we shouldn't go *too* far in making the transition smooth and ensuring continuity of experience. He suggests that some *dis*continuity is needed so that learners are aware that they have risen to the next level of education.

Try the MI ice-breakers on the opposite page.

...IN ACTION

Speed learn

1. Ask your learners to complete an MI questionnaire (see page 35), and discuss the results. Identify areas of strength.
2. Arrange seats into pairs of straight lines facing each other, so that each learner sits facing one other person.
3. Give learners on the right-hand side 30 seconds to share their name and strengths with the person opposite.
4. After 30 seconds, everyone on the right moves to the next chair and repeats their introduction to their new partner (The end person comes round to the start of the line.)
5. Repeat this several times, then ask learners on the left to share and move in the same way.

MI bingo (adapt for the age of learner)

1. Give each learner a copy of the bingo card below.
2. Challenge them to find ten different people: one for each skill.
3. They should write that person's name in the square on the card.
4. The aim is for *every* player to get a completed card – *not* just the first one.

Plays a musical instrument _____	Can sing, in tune and in time, to an audience _____
Can play chess and/or do sudoku quickly _____	Can persuade parents to do things _____
Can name at least ten different plants _____	Can talk his/her way out of trouble _____
Can organise friends for a trip to town _____	Can work out how others are feeling _____
Plays a sport well _____	Can write and edit web pages _____

Training and consultancy

If your role in the world of education involves speaking at conferences; running workshops and seminar days; or training, consultancy, advice and inspection, then there are two main approaches to using MI in this work:

- Including MI as content in your training or support.
- Using MI to deliver your training or support.

Ideally, do both!

You should do the first because it's important to inform your learners and delegates about this feature of 21st-century education (whether you're already an advocate of multiple intelligences or not).

The second is a way to model good practice.

Take the ideas on the facing page as starting points – adapt and develop them to meet the purpose of your training, the audience and the actual content.

> **TIP:**
> Use MI practice to teach MI theory.

...IN ACTION

The school report

- If appropriate and convenient, ask your delegates to bring one of their school reports* to the workshop.
- Check that they are comfortable doing so, then have them share sound bites and anecdotes from the reports.
- Now discuss the reports, looking through an MI lens. What intelligences strengths were missed? What intelligence weaknesses were emphasised?

MI celebrity double

- Ask delegates to complete an MI questionnaire and highlight three strengths.
- Give groups a selection of photographs of successful people who are in the public eye.
- Speculate on each celebrity's three strongest intelligences.
- Match yourself to a celebrity who shares (or nearly shares) your three intelligences strengths.
- You have found your MI celebrity double!

Wrong size shoes

- Set up five or six simple activities – each linked to an intelligence (for example, set up a discussion group, create a song, draw a picture, identify plants and animals).
- Ask delegates to identify their very weakest intelligence.
- Ask delegates to carry out an activity that requires this intelligence.
- Share experiences.
- Tell delegates that being taught in a way that doesn't match your intelligence strengths, for some people, can be as uncomfortable as wearing shoes a couple of sizes too small day after day.

---

* An alternative to delegates' own reports is *Could Do Better: School Reports of the Great and Good* edited by Catherine Hurley (Simon & Schuster).

Involving parents and the community

Page 40 suggests how you can *inform* parents and carers about multiple intelligences in school. By taking this a stage further and *involving* them, you can mine the rich seam of their experiences and their uses of the different intelligences.

For you, your learners and the school, MI offers the chance to personalise teaching and learning in a manageable way, and provides a framework for raising self-esteem. And if you are able to arrange an MI workshop, you should see further positive outcomes for parents, such as:

- They are inspired to find out more.
- They view their children and themselves in a more optimistic way.
- They understand that there are many ways to support their children's learning.
- They see their own school experience and working lives in a new light.

The activity idea on the following page, which involves parents' expert skills directly in a lesson, is very well suited to school governors as well as parents.

TIP:
At a workshop, strike while the iron's hot to enlist parents' help – as the workshop ends, during the coffee and chat, and by letter the following day.

...IN ACTION

Careers illustrate the use of different intelligences. Invite parents as MI expert guests to a question-and-answer session.

Make sure your learners have relevant questions and know how to welcome a guest. Likewise, check your organisation's procedures for having visitors work with students, and be prepared to support your guest during the session.

Expert guest	Typical intelligences being demonstrated	
Builder, plumber, carpenter, etc.	Bodily Visual	Logical
Cleaner	Naturalist Visual Bodily	Interpersonal Intrapersonal
Doctor	Interpersonal Intrapersonal	Linguistic Logical
Hairdresser	Interpersonal Visual Bodily	Logical Intrapersonal
Long-distance lorry driver	Intrapersonal Visual	Bodily
Checkout operator	Intrapersonal Interpersonal	Logical
Dancer	Bodily Musical	Intrapersonal
Pilot	Visual Bodily	Logical Intrapersonal
Priest/Imam, etc.	Existential Interpersonal	Intrapersonal Linguistic

IDEA...

Raising boys' achievement

Not all boys need their standards of achievement raising, but statistics in the UK do reveal a consistently worrying gap between male and female exam scores.

There are many issues around this discrepancy, for example:

- Society – sends mixed messages to boys.
- Culture – says it's not 'macho' to work hard.
- Schools – don't provide what boys need.
- Men/fathers – some aren't there/don't have time.
- Brains – are wired differently from girls'.

All these (and more) are reasons, but not excuses, for boys' underachievement.

If the following thoughts about learning are typical of boys, what MI-inspired activities should we provide for them?

> I want to talk to my mates rather than read a book.

> I can't keep still like they want me to.

> What's school for anyway?

> I can't focus on what the teachers are telling me to do.

> I want to do things not hear about them.

As a very rough rule of thumb, boys need to:

- Do/move/touch
- Talk
- Look;

rather than:

- Listen
- Keep still
- Write.

...IN ACTION

Big wheel

This activity hooks into linguistic, visual and kinesthetic intelligences in an attempt to meet (some) boys' learning needs:

1. Arrange eight (or six or ten) seats as follows:

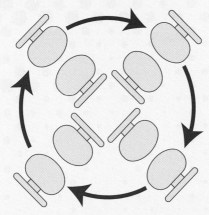

2. Learners sit in a big wheel so that everyone is facing a partner.

3. Give each learner an image related to the learning objective (for geography, for example: a series of photographs of natural features; for MFL: scenes from daily life in a European city).

4. Give learners sitting in the inner wheel one minute to describe their image to their partner.

5. After the minute, learners in the outer wheel move round one place clockwise, and listen to their new partner for a minute.

6. Repeat until learners in the inner wheel have described their image four times.

7. Inner and outer wheels swap places and repeat the activity.

8. The roles of inner and outer wheels can be adapted for different subjects, stimulus material, need and so on. For example, for revision, as role play, or in interviews.

Supporting new teachers

There's a good chance that your organisation includes one or more teachers who are just starting out. If your organisation is a school, there's an even higher chance that these new teachers will have one issue topmost in their minds:

Behaviour management!

MI can provide an alternative view of classroom misbehaviour and an indirect but effective route to solving some of the problems.

Disruptive genius

Liz Flaherty from Cove Secondary School in Farnborough uses MI theory to think about disruptive behaviour in class. She believes that each of the intelligences, and combinations of them, can be the cause of different 'problem' behaviours.

Classroom management

Effective classroom management is the key to managing disruptive behaviour. If you address only the behaviour, then you're fighting the symptom, not the cause.

In practice, this means managing the classroom so that opportunities for misbehaviour are minimised. One way to do this is to match learning activities to learner MI strengths – make the lessons attractive, engaging and meaningful (also see Chapter 5).

...IN ACTION

Consider the possibility that some learners may not be deliberately difficult or non-compliant. Perhaps their intelligence strengths are not being fully used. Look out for these 'symptoms'.

Intell.	Manifestation as 'disruptive' behaviour
V/L	• Checks repeatedly what s/he has been asked to do • Chats as s/he completes a task • Has difficulty in maintaining 'exam conditions'
L/M	• Asks why • Seeks clarifications: how much to write, how many questions there are, how much time is left
M/R	• Hums quietly • Taps out rhythms • Uses an iPod
V/S	• Needs to sit in 'his'/'her' seat • Likes personal area not to be obstructed • Behaves worse if in a strange room
B/K	• Fidgets and finds it hard to sit still • Plays with equipment • Leaves seat at any opportunity • Touches other pupils
Inter	• Likes to know what is going on in others' lives • Chats about social life • Easily distracted by other people • Likes to be the centre of attention
Intra	• Keeps head down • Reluctant to participate in class • Thinks things through for him/herself • Doesn't seek out the company of peers
N	• Finds it hard to be in an enclosed room • Often looks out of the window • Likes to be close to the door

IDEA...

MI around the world

General points

- As a rule of thumb, places adopt MI principles to the extent that they think progressively and recognise and embrace differences between individuals.
- Gardner continues to be amazed that since 1983 his idea still flourishes across the world and is used creatively by both education and business organisations.
- He especially likes discovering innovative combinations of MI with other ideas in which he believes.
- He advises that people should only use MI ideas if they help to meet their goals. If not, do something else.
- More thoughts on global MI appear in *Multiple Intelligences Around the World* (Basic Books), which includes a chapter by this author.

China

- Very enthusiastic and large-scale uptake of MI practices.
- There are over 100 books in Chinese about MI.

Thailand (Bangkok) and Brazil

- Two places where learning a foreign language is very important.
- MI (as a way of thinking) has been used to get children reading, speaking and understanding more than one language.

Philippines

- An MI school in Manilla gives out eight national awards inspired by MI and Gardner's *GoodWork Project* for ethical, meaningful, high-quality work.

In 2006 Howard Gardner addressed over 300 educational researchers in a session called 'MI in Global Perspective'. Educators from Brazil, China, England and Turkey shared the stage as Gardner related how his theory has been both used and abused worldwide. Here is a summary of his observations.

...IN ACTION

Ireland (Dublin) and Spain (Barcelona)

- Two places with schools which focus on 'education for understanding' (rather than 'knowledge for recall').
- MI plays a big part in their practices.

Italy (Reggio Emilia)

- The origin of the ethical, popular and timely Reggio Emilia approach to pre-school education.
- One of the key ideas in this approach is 100 Languages of Children, an idea that dovetails perfectly with the intelligences.

Denmark (Danfoss Universe)

- A theme park with 50 interactive exhibits designed with and inspired by MI.
- Open to families and for business training.

Russia and East Asia

- Not much interest in MI in cultures that tend to want everyone to turn out the same.
- Some interest from rebel and maverick educators.

UK and France

- Some interest, but countries feel they have little to learn from the USA.

USA

- The New City School in St Louis opened the world's first MI school library in 2005.
- The USA still has the capacity to inspire practices elsewhere, even though its current educational thinking in general is anything but progressive.

FURTHER READING

MI books and websites

Frames of Mind; Intelligence Reframed and *Multiple Intelligences: New Horizons* by Howard Gardner (all Basic Books)

MI in the Elementary School: a Teacher's Toolkit by Susan Baum, Julie Viens and Barbara Slatin (Teachers' College Press)

Becoming a Multiple Intelligences School by Tom Hoerr (ASCD)

Multiple Intelligences in Practice by Mike Fleetham (Network Continuum)

The Best of Multiple Intelligences Activities (Teacher Created Materials)

MI profiling: www.bgfl.org/multipleintelligences; www.thinkingclassroom.co.uk; www.miresearch.org

A world-leading MI school: www.newcityschool.org

Howard Gardner's Project Zero and Project Spectrum research: www.pz.harvard.edu; http://www.pz.gse.harvard.edu/project_spectrum.php

Gardner's GoodWork Project: http://www.old-pz.gse.harvard.edu/Research/GoodWork.htm

Additional resources

How Children Succeed by Paul Tough (HMH)

The Element by Ken Robinson (Allen Lane)

Could Do Better: School Reports of the Great and Good edited by Catherine Hurley (Simon & Schuster)

IQ and g: www.intelligencetest.com

Reggio Emilia in the USA: www.reggiochildren.it

About the author

Mike Fleetham is an education consultant and executive coach, who works with schools to help make learning more effective and more enjoyable. He specialises in the practical classroom application of established theories, including Multiple Intelligences. He has collaborated with Prof. Howard Gardner and colleagues from around the world to produce a comprehensive survey of how MI is used in different educational contexts.

Mike's website www.thinkingclassroom.co.uk offers free resource downloads that are currently used by teachers in over 120 countries and territories.

"I often find that entrepreneurs think my theory is great. My interpretation is that they are people who weren't considered that smart in school because they didn't have good notation skills – you know, moving little symbols around."

Howard Gardner

"Everybody is a genius. But if you judge a fish by its ability to climb a tree, it will live its whole life believing that it is stupid."

Albert Einstein

Other titles in the series

Boys and Writing by Steve Bowkett

Building Learning in Mathematics by Stephanie Prestage, Els De Geest and Anne Watson

Creating Enquiring Minds by Sara Stanley

Emotional Intelligence by Steve Bowkett

Involving Parents in Schools by Bill Lucas

Learning Styles and Personalized Teaching by Barbara Prashnig

Making Learning Fun by UFA National Team

Newly Qualified Teachers by Henry Liebling

Raising Boys' Achievement by Gary Wilson

Successful Provision for Able and Talented Children by Barry Teare